T
re
b
R
st

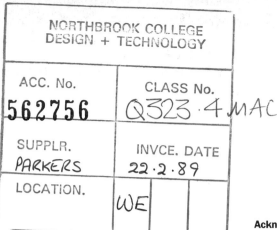
Factual Advisers

Anna Davin
History Workshop Journal Editor
London

Tidings P. Ndhlovu
Economist
University of East Anglia

Series and Book Editor: Nicole Lagneau
Teacher Panel: Paula Bartley, Hilary Kemeny, Sue Wilkinson
Designer: Ewing Paddock
Production: Rosemary Bishop
Picture Research: Caroline Mitchell

A MACDONALD BOOK

© Macdonald & Company (Publishers) Ltd 1987

First published in Great Britain in 1987 by Macdonald
& Company (Publishers) Ltd, London & Sydney
A BPCC plc company
All rights reserved

Printed and bound by Henri Proost
Turnhout, Belgium

Macdonald & Co (Publishers) Ltd
Greater London House
Hampstead Road
London NW1 7QX

British Library Cataloguing in Publication Data
Macdonald, Fiona
   Working for equality — (Women history-makers).
   1. Civil rights movements — History — 20th century — Juvenile
   literature
   2. Women social reformers — History — 20th century — Juvenile
   literature
   I. Title   II. Series
   323.4   JC571
   ISBN 0-356-13122-X
   ISBN 0-356-13123-8 Pbk

Acknowledgements

We would like to thank Virago Press
for permission to quote from *The
Cause* by R. Strachey, 1978; Also
to Macmillan for permission to
quote from *Race, Reform and
Rebellion* by M. Marable, 1984; to
Pennsylvania State University Press
for permission to quote from *Black
Women in Nineteenth Century
American Life* by B. J. Loewenberg
& R. Bogen, 1976; to Penguin
Books for permission to quote from
Part of My Soul by Winnie Mandela,
1985 and *Strong Minded Women*
by J. Horowitz Murray, 1984; to
The Feminist Press for permission
to quote from *Black Foremothers*
by D. Sterling, 1979; to Russell &
Volkening, Inc. for permission to
quote from *My Soul is Rested* by
H. Raines, 1977.

We acknowledge the source of
quotes from the following:
*Women and the American Labor
Movement* by P. S. Foner, Free
Press, 1980.
When and Where I Enter by
P. Giddings, Bantam Books, 1985.
Call Me Woman by E. Kuzwayo,
The Women's Press, 1985.
Quote from an article called *Hair
Trigger Justice* by Robert B. Cullen
and Ray Wilkinson, Newsweek
Magazine (16/9/85 issue).
Mother of a Nation by Nancy
Harrison, Grafton/Collins, 1984.
In addition we should like to thank
those writers and publishers whom
we have not been able to contact
and whose work is reprinted in this
publication. We invite them to
contact us.

Illustrations:

Paul Cooper, page 32

Photographs

Afrapix/Network: 5, 35B.
Associated Press: back cover, 29T,
30.
Eric Auerbach: 29B.
BBC Hulton: 17T.
BBC Hulton/Bettmann Archive: 24,
25B, 27.
Camera Press: Cover BL, 36.
Orde Eliason/Link: 39T.
Mary Evans Picture Library: 12, 14,
15, 16, 21B, 32.
Mary Evans Picture Library/Fawcett
Library: 20.
IDAF: 9R, 37B & T, 38, 39B, 40,
41.
Imperial War Museum: 21T.
Macdonald Library: 10T, 19T, 42.
Mansell Collection: 17B.
National Museum of Labour
History: 19B.
Network/Marc Vanappelghem: 35T.
Popperfoto: Cover TL, 6-7, 10B, 11,
22, 23, 26, 31T & B, 33, 34.
David Redfern Photography/Beryl
Bryden: 25T.
Rex Features: Cover R.
Schlesinger Library, Radcliffe
College: 9L, 28.
John Topham Picture Library: 8, 13,
18.

Cover captions:
Front top: London's suffragettes demonstrating, 1910,
(see pages 10–21).
Bottom: Bussing in Boston, USA (see glossary page 44 and
page 23).
Right: Winnie Mandela (b. 1934) (see page 32–4).
Back cover: Rosa Parks (b. 1914) (see page 30).

WORKING FOR EQUALITY

Fiona Macdonald

Macdonald

About this book

Half the people in the world are women. So why do women appear so seldom in books on history? One reason is that until recently, history has been mainly about public events; in the past many people thought that women should not take part in these. But, all the same, some women defied what people thought and worked to change society for the better. Their public achievements made history or would have done if historians had remembered to take notice of them.

In the past, many historians have shared the traditional general view that a woman's real place was at home, serving her family. If they found proof to the contrary, they often didn't recognize it, or ignored it. (The only women they could never ignore were female rulers.) Often, too, they summed up women's achievements in a couple of sentences, or a footnote in small print. The books in this series aim to put the women history-makers back where they belong: in the world they helped change, and in the way that we remember that world.

The three women you will read about here belonged to the world of the late 19th and early 20th centuries, but they lived in different countries. One, called Millicent Garrett Fawcett, was British; another, Rosa Parks, is American. The third, Winnie Mandela, is South African. This book shows you what they have in common.

How to use this book

When studying the past, all historians try to go back to what the people of the past actually wrote and said. In the sections of this book marked **'Witness'**, you can read some of the things said by people living at the time of Millicent Garrett Fawcett, Rosa Parks and Winnie Mandela, and comments from the women themselves. Keep a look-out for these, and look out, too, for the sections marked **'Action'**. These will raise questions about how history was written in the past. They will ask you to examine some of the source material in the witness section more closely, and to think about why these women history-makers acted as they did.

During the 1960s mass protests forced the government to take action against racial discrimination in the south. In March 1965, 15,000 people assembled outside the White House in Washington DC. They were protesting against racial discrimination in Alabama.

Contents

Women and history

Throughout history, few societies have been able to guarantee equality for all their members. Some societies have been divided into different classes, where how much money a person has, or what family they come from, determines how important they are. Some societies have been divided by religion, or by colour, or by the types of job people do. In many societies, people have believed that women are not equal with men, and that they should not, therefore, play a part in public life.

All societies have a set of rules by which they are governed. Sometimes these rules are written down in a special document, such as the American Constitution. In other countries, like Britain or South Africa, these rules take the form of laws passed by Parliament. They usually reflect the beliefs of the most powerful people in society. Anyone who wants to change the rules, because they believe that they are unfair, has to persuade these powerful people (usually the government) to change their minds. They can do this by arguing their case, or by peaceful campaigning. Or they can try to influence the people with power by defying the rules and breaking the law. If enough people protest in this way against a law which they believe to be unjust, then they may be able to force the government to change it. But they also run the risk of being arrested and put in prison for breaking the law.

This book looks at three women who have campaigned for greater equality within their own societies, and who have tried to get various governments to change the law by very different means. Millicent Garrett Fawcett lived in Victorian England, where women were thought to be incapable of making sensible decisions about politics. She fought to persuade the government to allow women to have equal rights with men to vote. Rosa Parks lives in mid–20th century America, and has campaigned to secure equal rights for the black and white peoples of the USA. Winnie Mandela lives in South Africa, where the rules that govern society are grossly unfair to black people. She has fought for a change in these rules, and for a new government for South Africa which will try to ensure equality for all its citizens, whatever the colour of their skin.

These women have chosen different ways of campaigning, according to their circumstances, their beliefs and their temperaments. But, as this book will show you, they have all worked for equality.

Millicent Garrett Fawcett, 1847–1929, British campaigner for votes for women. Born into a wealthy family in Victorian England, she became actively involved in her husband's political activities. She soon began to campaign for her own 'cause', the right of women to be allowed to vote on equal terms with men.

Rosa Parks, born in 1914 into a working-class family in the southern states of America. She defied a local law which treated black people unfairly, to prove that the law was unjust. The Supreme Court of the USA finally upheld her view. Her example inspired other blacks to stand up for their rights, and a great mass movement was born.

Nomzamo Winnie Mandela, born in 1934, came from a family of local chiefs in South Africa. Her concern for her fellow Africans, and her marriage to Nelson Mandela, led to her campaign for the abolition of the unjust apartheid system and her involvement in the struggle for equality between black and white people in South Africa.

Derby Day

It was Derby Day, 1913. The crowds at Epsom race-course were enjoying a good day out. All morning, horse-drawn omnibuses had carried cheerful passengers from London out to the course on Epsom downs. The grass was dotted with lively groups of picnickers; there were buskers and ballad-singers, pickpockets and card-sharps, gypsies telling fortunes and bookies shouting the odds on all the different horses. Excited children ran everywhere, pleased to be in the open air after the smog of London.

It was nearly time for the races to start. Jockeys whispered threats and encouragements to their eager, nervous horses. The spectators tried to get close to the track to catch a glimpse of the favourite. Those who could afford it paid for a seat in the grandstand.

'They're off!' The horses sprang forward. 'They're coming!' The crowd pressed up against the rails. Then, before anyone could stop her, a woman dashed out on to the course and threw herself under the pounding hooves of the leading horse. It was hard to see what happened next. The frightened jockey cried out in alarm; the startled horse swerved, staggered and fell heavily. The woman lay very, very still. A few days later, she was dead.

What caused that woman to commit suicide in so dramatic a way? Was she mad? Or was she ill? Why choose Derby Day, which always attracted vast crowds, and was a favourite day out for Londoners and their families? Why did she throw herself under a horse? The newspapers said she was a suffragette, who was campaigning for votes for women. How did she

Above, a member of the Women's Social and Political Union (the militant wing of the votes for women campaign). She is being arrested after trying to interrupt a royal wedding in 1913.

Below, the crowded scene at Epsom racecourse where Emily Wilding Davidson committed suicide to draw attention to the suffragettes' demands for equal votes for women.

A peaceful open-air meeting organized by the National Union of Women's Suffrage Societies, the non-militant campaigners led by Millicent Garrett Fawcett.

imagine that killing herself would help her cause? Throughout history, men and women have been prepared to die for their beliefs. That woman did not see her suicide as a negative act. It was the ultimate sacrifice she could make to help the cause she supported. She chose Derby Day as the place to do it in order to get maximum publicity for her beliefs.

She was a suffragette, a supporter of the Women's Social and Political Union, (WSPU), founded by Emmeline Pankhurst in 1903. Suffragettes believed that women should have equal rights with men to vote for Members of Parliament. In the 19th century the vote had gradually been extended to middle class and skilled working class men. But the idea of votes for women was still fiercely opposed by most politicians. Women had been campaigning for the right to vote long before 1903. Some preferred to put forward their views by slow and patient argument and discussion. They were known as suffragists. Millicent Garrett Fawcett, their leader, described their approach as being 'like the movement of a glacier'. In contrast,

some of the WSPU suffragettes saw the campaign to get the vote for women as, almost literally, a war against men who wanted to keep all political power in their own hands. 'Liberty was never won by pleading, and cannot be purchased,' wrote Theresa Billington Greig, a leading WSPU member. There had been many violent clashes between suffragettes and the forces of law and order in the months before the Derby Day suicide. WSPU members had staged noisy, disruptive protests at many public meetings. They had marched and shouted and had even chained themselves to the railings outside government buildings. They had refused to pay taxes or to recognize the authority of the courts. Suffragettes had been beaten up and roughly arrested, imprisoned and even forcibly fed when they went on hunger strike.

Why should women's demand for political equality provoke such a response? To answer this, we need to look at the position of women in society during the 19th century, and what the suffragettes' opponents thought a woman's role should be.

WITNESS

'The vote is the symbol of freedom and equality. Any class which is denied the vote is branded an inferior class. Women's disenfranchisement is to them a perpetual lesson in servility, and to men it teaches arrogance and injustice where their dealings with women are concerned. The inferiority of women is a hideous lie which has been enforced by law and woven into the British Constitution, and it is quite hopeless to expect reform between the relationship of the sexes until women are politically enfranchised.'
Source: C. Pankhurst, *The Great Scourge and How to End It,* 1913.

Working women

Before the 19th century, it was taken for granted that all women had a variety of jobs to perform, as well as bearing and bringing up children. Poor women laboured in the fields, weeding and harvesting crops. At home, they cooked, cleaned, looked after their families, cared for the sick, reared poultry and perhaps a pig, made and mended clothes, and tried to earn a little cash by spinning or knitting.

Women who were more comfortably off, like the wives of substantial farmers or prosperous shopkeepers, also worked hard. Even with servants to help them, the task of running a household of perhaps ten people kept women busy from dawn to late at night. Among their tasks were: cleaning and furnishing a large house, providing food for hungry employees twice a day, brewing, baking, cheese-making, preserving fruit, preparing simple herbal remedies, teaching servants how to carry out their tasks, keeping household accounts and entertaining the family's visitors.

If their husband was an important man in the local community, they might also have to undertake 'public' duties, such as visiting the poor or sick, or helping to find good places for local children as servants or apprentices. Even among the wealthy, where women had no need to perform hard physical work, a husband expected his wife to act as a gracious hostess. This meant that she had to entertain important guests so as to further his business or political career. She was also responsible for the smooth running of large households in London and in the country. Many wealthy women supported a large number of good causes.

In the 18th century, many upper class women made strenuous efforts to educate themselves, and took an active interest in the works and ideas of writers, artists and philosophers of their age. There were many amateur, and a few professional, women writers. Some women wrote novels or plays, others wrote pioneering works which discussed women's role in society. Women from all classes made a name for

This picture, drawn in 1871, shows Elizabeth Fry, the great prison reformer. Like many wealthy women, she was brought up to think of charitable visiting as part of her duty. She was so appalled by the conditions she found in prisons that she devoted her whole life to trying to make life better for the prisoners.

themselves as skilled performers. Famous women singers and actors were celebrated throughout Europe for their talents and achievements.

Although women were playing an important role in society, the value of their contribution was never publicly acknowledged. Men did not regard women as their equals in law or in practice. But during the 18th century, some women did begin to demand equality with men. As Mary Wollstonecraft wrote in 1792, 'Who made man the exclusive judge, if women partake with him the gift of reason?' Why are 'women excluded without having a voice?'

Over 100 years later, the suffragettes were still trying to convince men of the rightness of this argument: that women had a valuable contribution to make to politics. Christabel Pankhurst wrote in *The Suffragette,* in November 1913, 'Social justice will never be established until the man's point of view, of which our present social system is the expression, is corrected by the women's point of view.'

Why, after so long an interval, was it necessary for the suffragettes to repeat Mary Wollstonecraft's arguments? What had happened to women during the so-called 'century of progress'? Why were women still not being treated as equals by men?

Traditional, home-based work, in 1905. The whole family works together to earn a living. These workers are baiting fishing lines outside their home near Whitby, Yorkshire. This job was usually done by older women and retired men. Younger women worked down by the quayside, packing fish, and younger men went to sea.

WITNESS

Here Martineau, a journalist, is arguing that women who fulfil the traditional female role of bringing up children have a very important part to play in shaping the society of the future. For this reason, mothers should 'think and speak wisely'.

'The time has not come which certainly will come when women who are practically concerned in political life will have a voice in making the laws which they are to obey; but every woman who can think and speak wisely, and bring up children soundly, in regard to the rights and duties of society is advancing the time when the interests of women will be represented as well as those of men.'
Source: Harriet Martineau, *Illustrations of Political Economy,* 1832–1834.

'Unwomanly' women

Patterns of work were re-organized for both men and women during the course of the 19th century. But this did not help women's fight for equality with men. Gradually, large numbers of people moved from the country to the new industrial towns in search of work. This meant that workers became cut off from their old communities. Men and women no longer worked together in farms and workshops. In the eyes of most factory owners, women were simply pairs of hands to be used as required. Women could be paid lower wages than men, and rarely got supervisory jobs. Male factory workers used to help and support each other at work, but they tended to ignore women.

When trade unions were formed to fight for better conditions, many of them were unwilling to accept female members. They feared that women might take their jobs from them. Separate women's unions were set up, but they did not always receive much co-operation from their male counterparts. In 1887 the Trades Union Congress (TUC) declared that 'men's wives should be in their proper sphere at home, instead of being dragged into competition of livelihood with the great strong men of the world.'

Women with young families or sick relatives often took in sewing or laundry or piece-work from factories to do at home. They were usually paid extremely low wages, and this had the effect of making their labour seem unimportant. And no-one questioned the inequality caused by working women doing, in effect, several jobs: cooking and housework and child care in addition to their paid employment.

It was not only members of the TUC who regarded factory work as somehow 'unfeminine'. 'Women working in factories disturbs the order of nature . . .' said Anthony Ashley Cooper, later Lord Shaftesbury, an influential social reformer, in a speech in Parliament in 1844. Middle class men also looked at working women as examples of an inferior species. Factory 'girls' were thought to be loud and boisterous. Like prostitutes, who were often forced on to the streets through poverty, they were not thought of as real women. They did not count in society. There was no reason to give them the vote. Unmarried women who worked as servants were thought unworthy to take part in the running of the country. The servant was treated like an irresponsible child by her employer. Her

A cycle-manufacturing workshop in Coventry, in 1895. Women work at assembly benches under the eye of a male supervisor (far left). Skilled workers like these earned lower wages than men. An increasing number of women worked in factories; they were no longer tied exclusively to the home. But those who went out to work were likely to be unmarried.

A trade union demonstration, in 1877. Women were active in the trade union movement. Some joined male unions, others set up women-only unions. The attitudes of male trade unionists towards women varied a great deal. Some supported women in their fight for equality. Others feared that women would compete with them for their jobs. Men's fight to be paid a 'family wage' re-enforced the idea of the man as breadwinner, and tended to make women's work seem less important.

clothes, food and even her bed-time were all chosen for her. She could certainly not be trusted with the vote! In 1861, about 2.7 million women over 15, or about ¼ of the female population, were in paid employment. Even so, the contribution of such a large number of women to the country's economy was not considered valuable enough to give women a say in the running of its affairs. In spite of male opposition, strong-minded women kept up their campaigns for an improvement in women's status and treatment. Not all these campaigns were concerned with the vote. In the 1850s, women were actively involved in the fight against slavery. In the 1850s and '60s, they protested against high food prices and the suffering they caused among the poor.

Women also campaigned for changes in the law regarding child custody, divorce and married women's property. Josephine Butler led a daring campaign to end the government's persecution of prostitutes, and to provide better care for them. Many new trade unions for women were founded in the 1870s. Women became active helpers in local political campaigns after the vote was granted to a large number of men in 1885.

All these women demonstrated in their daily working lives and in their campaigns to improve society that they could be hard-working, careful, clear-thinking, organized and responsible. But the opposition to votes for women remained strong. Public (male) opinion remained convinced that a woman's place was in the home. How did such a limited view of women, which was daily contradicted by the evidence in front of men's eyes, come to be so powerful?

" WITNESS

A rather exaggerated, sentimental description of different classes of women in Victorian England. Note that both types of women are presented as helpless, either trapped in luxury or weighed down by hopeless poverty:

'On one side I see women who are lapped in every luxury which the hands of loving fathers and husbands can give them . . . they never know the great realities of life. . . And then I see on the other side . . . perhaps there are a million or so — who are very poor, struggling sorrowfully, painfully, often failing from pressure of want of employment, or of grinding oppression and cruelty from those whose duty it is to protect and cherish them . . . they have to fight a far harder battle than ever falls to the lot of man . . . there is wrong, grievous wrong somewhere.'
Source: speech calling for votes for women by Frances Power Cobbe, 1876.

'When . . . we ask why the existence of one half of the species should be merely ancillary to that of the other — why each woman should be a mere appendage to a man, allowed to have no interests of her own that there may be nothing to compete in her mind with his interests and pleasure, the only reason that can be given is, men like it.'
Source: Harriet Taylor, The Emancipation of Women, Westminster Review, 1851.

In the 19th century, 'Some women were considered too frail to walk alone in the streets, while others were working underground in coal mines.'
Source: Comment by the modern American historian, Janet Horowitz Murray, in her book Strong-Minded Women, 1982.

"

The 'domestic angel'

'A woman is courted and wedded as an angel and yet denied the dignity of a rational and moral being ever after' (Barbara Bodichon c. 1854).

'A lady . . . does not work' (Margaretta Grey, 1853).

Throughout history, women have been regarded by some men with a sort of 'double vision'. On the one hand, men have lived, worked, and shared the experiences of everyday life with real, flesh-and-blood women. On the other hand, they have constructed a series of 'ideal' images to which women of the time have been expected to conform. (Men construct ideal types for themselves, too, of course; just think of the old-fashioned 'stiff-upper-lip' British hero). Sometimes women have been happy to go along with one or other of these idealized versions of themselves. At other times women have been too poor or exhausted by overwork to have felt able to complain.

Women's views about these ideal images have often not been recorded in history books, because no men living at the time thought them worth noting. But for the Victorian period, we are fortunate in having a large amount of evidence which records the views of both men and women about the contemporary ideal woman. To many Victorian men, their ideal woman was a 'domestic angel'. She lived only for her husband and family, her activities were largely confined to the house, and the only way in which she could hope to achieve anything was by 'doing good'. She was not meant to be concerned with the discussion of ideas, or politics, or any social issues outside the home. Only a limited amount of charity work was allowed. She was, of course, married. Single women were regarded as failures or as a social threat. But she was not expected to enjoy sexual relations with her husband; she was too 'pure' for that. Her clothing, with long skirts, fragile materials and tightly-corseted waists, emphasised her delicacy and her dependence on her husband. She was clearly not dressed for work!

A wife should be docile, charming and an excellent hostess. Once she was married, all her property and most of her civil rights were lost to her husband. Legally, she was under his 'command and control'.

This way of treating women developed and grew more powerful as the structure of 19th century society changed. It reflected the hopes and fears of the new middle class, which more than doubled in size between 1840–1880. The middle class in England wanted to prevent popular revolutions of the kind which had taken place in Europe in the 1790s and

No. 15.]   SATURDAY, AUGUST 7, 1858.   [ONE PENNY.

WITNESS

An educational reformer looks at changes in middle-class society: *'Within these few years a vast and sweeping change has taken place, of unprecedented rapidity, causing a reaction from this doctrine of idleness and dependence as essential to ladyhood towards the opposite* extreme, of work and independence as essential to honourable womanhood: work, meaning paid work and independence, meaning life apart from the home life, and free from the duties and constraining order of home.'
Source: Maria Grey, *Last Words to Girls: On Life in School and After School,* 1889.

Left, a cartoon making fun of 'advanced' women. Which of these activities would be thought by some men to be 'unwomanly'? Despite male opposition, groups of educated women continued to meet to discuss equal rights for women, including the right to vote.

How do you think these changes affected women's attitudes towards the vote, and men's attitudes towards women's demands to be considered as equals?

1840s. Such upheavals would destroy their new-found prosperity. Soon, middle class ideas of respectable family life, and of women's dependent role within the family, spread throughout society. Queen Victoria herself, though hardly weak or unintelligent, presented a model of a devoted wife and mother. Among working class women, the hope of achieving respectability often meant extra work and sacrifices in order to keep their homes, and the 'man of the house' obsessively clean, neat and 'proper'. Keeping wife and daughters away from any kind of work outside the home helped to establish the husband's importance in the eyes of the world.

Despite its importance to men's view of the world, the ideal of the 'domestic angel' was increasingly challenged towards the end of the 19th century. This challenge came from women, initially from the wealthy classes. They had time to think, to read and to discuss women's role in society. One of these women was Millicent Garrett Fawcett. Pioneering women struggled to win equal rights to education, or to train for the professions.

Many remarkable women campaigned to improve conditions for the poor, the sick, and those who were neglected by respectable society. Once ordinary women began to follow men into 'respectable jobs', such as shop assistant or clerk, it became increasingly hard to pretend that they did not have an important contribution to make to the world outside the home.

Above, a teacher and her class studying biology; the lesson is about 'roots'. Teaching was one way in which educated women could earn a living and become independent. When school became generally compulsory for all children in the 1870s, many women found jobs in the newly-opened state schools.

Left, upper class women taking tea in the garden. The two younger women have been playing tennis, even though they are dressed in tightly-waisted long frocks. Being a hostess helped an upper class woman to establish her family's place in polite society. Social contacts made this way might also help her husband's business.

17

A long struggle

Millicent Garrett Fawcett belonged to the remarkable generation of Victorian women who did so much to challenge the 'domestic angel' ideal, and to change the course of history. In her life dedicated to a cause, and in her belief in slow, steady but relentless pressure for social reform, she was typical of many who campaigned for an improvement in the condition of women. Like them, she believed that the right to vote would only be won when the position of women in society as a whole was made more equal with the position of men.

She was born Millicent Garrett, in 1847, one of ten children of a prosperous Suffolk shipowner. Her mother has been described as 'an intensely religious woman who worshipped her husband and was a domestic superwoman'. Millicent later said that her mother's powers of organization would have made her an excellent businesswoman. Her father was keenly interested in politics, and other members of the family circle also showed an interest in careers for women. Millicent often said that she felt called to struggle for votes for women 'from my cradle'. The following story, which may not be true, but which illustrates her sense of a lifetime's duty waiting for her, has been repeated many times since it first appeared in a history of the struggle for votes for women.

Millicent, her sister Elizabeth, and their friend Emily Davis, were sitting at home one evening. They were all very young. 'After going over all the great causes they saw about them, and in particular the women's cause, to which they were burning to devote their lives, Emily summed the matter up. 'Well, Elizabeth,' she said, 'it's quite clear what has to be done. I must devote myself to securing higher education, while you open the medical profession to women. After these things are done,' she added, 'we must see about getting the vote.' And then she turned to the little girl who was sitting quietly on her stool and said, 'You are younger than we are, Millie, so you must attend to that.' All three of these women were later to achieve their aims.

When Millicent was 20, she married Henry Fawcett, a respected academic and a Liberal MP. It was a happy marriage, and, for the times, an unusually equal one. Henry was blind, and for many years Millicent acted as his secretary. This, she said, was the beginning of her political education. She helped with his correspondence, read parliamentary papers, and summarized newspaper reports for him. They discussed important

Millicent Garrett Fawcett was typical of many educated women in Victorian times who devoted their lives to the struggle to improve women's position in society.

political issues together. Henry supported her career as a political writer, and attended meetings where she campaigned for votes for women.

Henry died in 1884, when Millicent was only 37. Their daughter (a brilliant mathematician) was nearly grown up. Millicent now found herself with few family responsibilities and more time to devote to the cause of votes for women. She soon won the respect of other campaigners for her intelligence and understanding of political matters. In 1890, she took over the leadership of the association of societies campaigning for votes for women. In 1897, this was re-named the National Union of Women's Suffrage Societies or 'Suffragists'. She remained President until 1918.

Throughout this period, she continued to remain committed to peaceful, legal means of campaigning, even though the more militant suffragettes urged her to join in their direct action campaign. During the war, she made an agreement with the government to stop campaigning, so that women could concentrate on

What a Woman may be, and yet not have the Vote

| MAYOR | NURSE | MOTHER | DOCTOR or TEACHER | FACTORY HAND |

What a Man may have been, & yet not lose the Vote

| CONVICT | LUNATIC | Proprietor of white Slaves | Unfit for Service | DRUNKARD |

A poster issued by women demanding the vote. It compares the useful work done by women with various groups of men who do not make any useful contribution to society. The men all have the right to vote, the women do not.

Right, an example of anti-suffragette propaganda. This cartoon suggests that a woman who spends her life campaigning for the right to vote is neglecting her 'proper' task of caring for her husband and family.

essential wartime work. In 1918, at long last, her efforts were partially rewarded. Women property-owners over 30 were given the right to vote. This small gain was not the result of a major change of heart among men in power. Nor, she believed, was it a reward for women's hard work during the war. Rather, she felt that women had been given a chance just to get a 'foot in the door' at a time when a major package of reforms in voting rights for men was being considered. The fight was not yet over.

Millicent Fawcett retired from active politics in 1919, when she was 72, although she continued to campaign until women were finally given the vote on an equal basis with men in 1928. She died in 1929, shortly after attending a public celebration, at which she was the guest of honour, to mark the appointment of the first-ever woman cabinet minister and the election of 14 women MPs. 'I have had,' she said, 'extra-ordinary good luck in having seen the struggle from the beginning.' She had maintained her dedication to the cause of votes for women for over 61 years.

A SUFFRAGETTE'S HOME

VOTES FOR WOMEN

AFTER A HARD DAY'S WORK!

Published by the Campaign Committee, National League for Opposing Woman Suffrage, Caxton House, Westminster. JOIN!

In the public eye

On 6 August, 1929, the *Manchester Guardian* published an obituary to Millicent Garrett Fawcett: 'There were three stages to the emancipation of women. The first was the long campaign of propaganda and organization, at the centre of which, patient, unwearying, and always hopeful, stood Dame Millicent. The second was the campaign of the militants . . . The third was war. Had there been no militancy and no war, the emancipation of women would have come, although more slowly. But without the faithful preparation of the ground over many years by Dame Millicent Fawcett and her colleagues neither militancy nor the war could have produced the crop.'

Throughout her political life, Millicent Garrett Fawcett had one aim, to win votes for women on an equal basis with men, by 'constitutional' means. Her single-minded vision did much to contribute to her success. Before joining in any other political activity, she thought carefully about how it might affect the cause. She has sometimes been criticized for not co-operating with the suffragettes in their militant struggle to achieve the same ends. She admired their physical courage and despised those women who were too lazy or timid to take part in any type of campaigning, but, none the less, she held to her chosen course of action.

She had two reasons for doing so. Firstly, as her *Guardian* obituary makes clear, she believed that her tactics were most likely to succeed, and she was proved right in the end. Secondly, the motivation which guided her actions was very different from that of many of the more radical social reformers and suffragettes. She did not see men as the enemy. In a speech in 1899, she argued that granting the vote to women was more than an end in itself. It was a chance to play an equal role with men in deciding the political future of the nation. It would improve women's minds by giving them the chance to make their own decisions. And this, in turn, she felt, would improve society as a whole. Men 'cannot know what women want and what suits the necessities of women's lives as well as women know these things themselves.'

Millicent Fawcett's views differed in other ways from many of the more progressive women campaigners of her day. She did not approve of free education, believing that the need to save up for school fees encouraged habits of thrift and sobriety among working class parents. She quarrelled with the famous welfare campaigner, Eleanor Rathbone, over her proposal to

Millicent Garrett Fawcett is speaking to a meeting in Edinburgh in 1925. After 1918, when the vote was given to women with property and over 30 years of age, Millicent Fawcett still continued to campaign for women to be given the vote on equal terms with men.

///ACTION

Imagine that you are a young woman living at home with your parents round about 1910. You have a married sister.

You hear about Millicent Garrett Fawcett's campaigns to give women the vote. From your experience, in a comfortable middle-class home, what do you think of her views?

What do you also think about the more militant suffragettes' activities? Write a letter to your married sister describing how you feel.

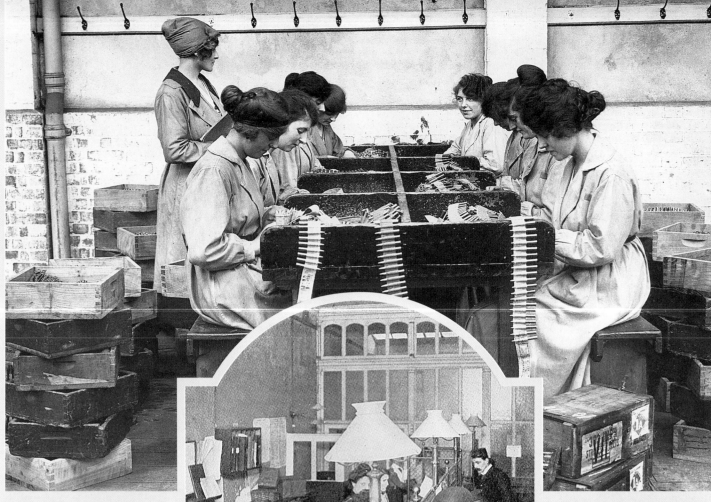

Above, women assembling machine-gun cartridges during the First World War. Women had started to work in munitions factories before the war, but in wartime they took over a large number of jobs to replace men who had gone overseas to fight. Women's wartime work helped to persuade politicians that some women could be trusted with the vote in 1918.

Left, post office clerks in 1902. As business boomed in the late 19th century, women began to play an increasing role in business life. Slowly, men began to accept women taking a more active part in the 'public' world. This change of attitude made it easier for some men to agree to women's demands to play an active part in politics, too.

pay family allowances to poor women. She had strong feelings for her country and opposed the formation of international women's groups during the 1914—1918 war, for fear that they might be unpatriotic.

However, despite these differences of character, background, political beliefs and tactics, Millicent Fawcett and the militant suffragettes were still fighting on the same side. Both groups wanted freedom for women to achieve their full potential. Both wanted an end to the idea that a 'real' woman's place was as a virtual prisoner in her home. Both wanted to see women using their vote to play an equal part with men in shaping a better society. The question 'how can political change be achieved?' is one that has been discussed by male politicians down the centuries. There is no right answer. Issues and circumstances change. It is to her great credit that Millicent Fawcett, fighting single-mindedly for her cause against tremendous opposition, found an answer that worked.

BIOGRAPHY

1847 Born into wealthy ship-owning family. One of ten children.
1867 Millicent married Henry Fawcett, a Liberal MP and an academic. Worked as his political secretary. Started to campaign for women to have the right to vote on equal terms with men. Insisted on peaceful campaigns.
1877 Began to campaign against Married Women's Property Act, and supported Josephine Butler's campaigns for fairer treatment of prostitutes. Both these campaigns worked for better treatment of women by male-dominated society.
1897 Founded National Union of Women's Suffrage Societies (NUWSS).
1903—1913 Disagreements with suffragettes over their campaigning methods.
1918 Welcomes limited grant of votes to women, but continues to campaign for votes to be given on an equal basis with men.
1924 Made Dame of the British Empire.
1928 Guest of honour at celebrations to mark final achievement of votes for all women over 21.
1929 Dies aged 81.

Born equal?

'In the spring of 1963, television cameras recorded unforgettable images: of Blacks turned into human pin-wheels by high-pressure streams from fire hoses; of snarling police dogs snapping at Black flesh; of a uniformed cop grinding his heel into the neck of a Black woman . . .' from *When and Where I Enter,* Paula Giddings, 1984.

How did these violent clashes come to take place, and in the United States of America, of all places? Didn't America pride itself on being the 'land of the free', where equal opportunities were available to all its citizens? What had driven some of these citizens to march and campaign, and why had other Americans reacted so brutally to these demonstrators? To understand the reasons behind the clashes that took place in many states of America during the 1960s, we must look back at the way in which black people had been treated in America since they first arrived there, and at the beginnings of the black people's struggle for equal rights as citizens of the USA. We must also look at how the refusal of Rosa Parks, an 'ordinary', poor, middle-aged, black woman to put up with unequal treatment, sparked off a political movement which changed a whole nation.

Black people in America, both men and women, had been campaigning for better treatment for nearly a hundred years, but, in the words of one black journalist: 'The Negro revolt is properly dated from the moment Mrs Rosa Parks said "No" to the bus driver's demand that she get up and let a White man have her seat . . .' How did so simple an action have such dramatic consequences?

66 WITNESS

'We hold these truths to be sacred and undeniable; that all men are created equal and independent, that from equal creation they derive rights inherent and inalienable, among which are the preservation of life and liberty, and the pursuit of happiness.'

Source: The American Declaration of Independence (a statement of the ideals that the new country planned to live by, after it had broken away from England and declared itself to be an independent nation in 1776). The draft was written by Thomas Jefferson (1743–1826).

After 1954, racial segregation in schools was illegal. But some southerners refused to respect the law. These pickets are outside a desegregated school in Nashville. Some whites believed that the blacks' demands for equal rights were communist inspired.

Rosa Parks' refusal to obey the bus driver's demand that she gave up her seat in December 1956 took place at a time when relations between black and white people in the USA were very tense. Rosa Parks herself had been involved in political campaigning for many years. From her own experience, she knew that racial prejudice was still widespread among ordinary white people. There had been a campaign of violence against blacks in some southern states, and black civil rights organizations were being examined by hostile investigators as part of the government's anti-communist campaign. Shops, cafés, and bars could still be signposted 'whites only'. Rosa Parks could be made to sit in a separate 'black' section of the bus because the law still allowed 'separate but equal' treatment of blacks. It was up to blacks to prove that the treatment they received was usually 'separate but inferior' by fighting expensive court cases.

Feelings had run very high over one famous court case not long before Rosa Parks made her protest. It was to do with the separate and unequal treatment of black and white people in schools. In 1954, the US Supreme

As the civil rights movement grew, so did white opposition to it, especially in the southern states. This picture shows a crowd of angry whites attacking two black men who attended an Independence Day rally in Atlanta, Georgia, in 1964.

Court had declared that it was illegal to force black and white children to attend separate schools or colleges, because 'separate facilities are inherently unequal'. But when black children attempted to go to former white schools, there were violent protests by white people. One black girl had acid thrown in her face by white pupils in her new school. Many local political leaders refused to accept the court's decision, and government troops had to be called in to protect the black school children.

Black people were outraged at this white refusal to obey the law. Civil rights organizations, especially the Congress of Racial Equality (CORE — founded in 1942, and including some white members) planned non-violent demonstrations to protest. It was against this background that Rosa Parks made her courageous gesture of defiance.

23

Slavery and after

Rosa Parks lived in Montgomery, Alabama, one of the southern states of America. Between 1861–1865, the northern and southern states fought a war. The southern states wanted to break away from the rest of the country and become independent. One of the causes of the quarrel between the states was a difference of opinion about slavery.

In the 17th and 18th centuries, the European colonists in America had imported thousands of black slaves, mostly from Western Africa, to work for them. Some slaves worked as labourers or as household servants, but most of them were used to cultivate the vast cotton plantations in the southern states. The white plantation owners regarded the slaves as their property. The slaves had to stay on the plantation where they were born, and work as their masters directed. They were cruelly punished if they tried to run away. They could be bought and sold in humiliating slave auctions. Some masters even forced slaves into marriages, so as to increase their future labour force by a 'breeding programme'.

Many people, in Europe as well as America, wanted to stop the hateful practice of slavery. Thomas Jefferson, one of America's most famous statesmen exclaimed after a visit to the southern state of Virginia, 'I tremble for my country when I reflect that God is just.' The northern states won the war, and slavery was officially abolished in America. But that did not make the southerners treat black people very much better. Freed slaves still did the worst jobs, lived in poor housing, and had less chance than white people of proper health care or education.

Here are two views of black American women of the 19th century. The first describes a famous woman journalist, Ida Wells. It was written by a black male journalist, who describes how impressed he was with her abilities: like Rosa Parks, Ida Wells fought a famous court case in 1884 over the right of black people to have equal use of public transport:
'She has become famous as one of the few of our women who handles a goose quill with a diamond point as handily as any of us men . . . she has plenty of nerve; she is smart as a steel trap; and she has no sympathy with humbug.'
Source: D. Sterling, *Black Foremothers*, 1979.

This is an extract from a speech made by Maria Stewart, a black feminist, to a group of black women in the 1830s:

'Do you ask what we can do? Unite and build a store of your own. Do you ask where is the money? We have spent more than enough for nonsense . . . We have never had an opportunity of displaying our talents; therefore the world thinks that we know nothing . . . Possess the spirit of men, bold and enterprising, fearless and undaunted. Sue for your rights and privileges.'
Source: B.J. Loewenberg and K. Bogin (eds.), *Black Women in 19th Century American Life,* 1976.

A black woman laundress on a plantation in Florida, USA. This was heavy and dirty work. Poor women were expected to work just as hard as men, and to care for husbands and children. Even educated black people found it hard to get good or well-paid jobs.

Conditions in the busy northern cities, like Chicago, were not much better. There, black factory workers were employed at lower rates of pay than their white colleagues, and black families lived in run-down ghetto areas, where public services, like clean water or sewers, were poorly-maintained or lacking altogether. But some black people did become prosperous by running businesses. A growing number of black people who had managed to get a good education became doctors, lawyers and journalists. Black people, both men and women, formed societies to campaign for equality and to do welfare work among the black community. But blacks still had to face abuse and sometimes violence from prejudiced white people. Black businesses were burned down, and innocent black people dragged from their homes and 'lynched' (executed) by angry mobs. In a famous incident in 1884, a well-known black woman journalist, Ida Wells, was thrown out of her seat in the 'ladies only' carriage of the train, and made to sit in the dirty and uncomfortable third class section. She took the railway company to court, and at first won her case. But when the railway appealed against the verdict, the highest court in the state overturned it. The railway company had acted lawfully, the court said. Blacks did not have equal rights with whites to sit where they chose.

After this, many black people felt that they had little chance of equal treatment with white people. Whatever the law might say, it seemed that it would always be possible for the white people who ran the country to use the law to support their own prejudiced views. And black people had to face other less violent but equally humiliating forms of discrimination. Many states denied them the right to vote. It was fair enough, thought the whites, for black people to succeed in certain roles, such as singers or dancers or sportsmen, because these roles were somehow 'naturally' suited to them. But there was no place for blacks in the mainstream of American society.

Below, black people often had to live in appalling housing, whether in the rural south or in the northern city ghettoes. This black preacher and his family have made a home, with their scanty possessions, in an abandoned schoolroom. This photo was taken in 1941.

Top, Billie Holliday, the famous blues singer. Her songs told of the sufferings of black people, as well as of her own tragic life. Even though black entertainers were accepted throughout the USA, they were still not treated as equals by many whites.

The black response

On pages 24–25 we saw how un-equally black people were treated in America during the decades following the Civil War. How did they respond? Understandably, different groups of black people found different ways of coping with discrimination.

Some, like the poor farm labourers in the south, had no choice. If they wanted to work, they had to put up with low wages and racial insults. The alternative was starvation. Many farmworkers moved to the big cities, to try and find better conditions, but they were mostly disappointed. Others tried to improve their chances by getting a better education, but this was hard, since the law still allowed separate schools for black and white pupils, and black schools were nearly always poorly-equipped, with large classes and few books. Often,

A black woman soldier member of the US troops fighting in Korea in 1950. Black soldiers fought alongside whites during World War II but often had to fight against racial prejudice too. It took many years to reduce discrimination within the armed forces.

children left school early to try and find work so as to contribute to the family income. Skilled workers could join a black trade union. Some of these, like the Brotherhood of Sleeping Car Porters, played an important part in making black people's views heard in national politics, even though many 'white' trade unions were unwilling to accept black members.

Other black people chose to take the roles 'allowed' to them by prejudiced whites. They were sometimes criticized for not opposing the system which denied job opportunities to blacks because of their colour. But black entertainers, like Louis Armstrong or Josephine Baker, in the 1930s and 1940s, performed 'black' music so well that they won world-wide respect. Black athletes, like Jesse Owens at the Olympic Games in Nazi Germany in the 1930s, used their success to make the point that, in sports, winning depends on how fast you can run, and not on the colour of your skin. At this time, too, a new black literature began to emerge, much of it written by women who described

This is a remark made by a famous black woman campaigner, Mary McLeod Bethune, who was active in politics in the 1930s – 1950s. It shows how black people wanted to take responsibility for their own destiny:

'The White man has been thinking for us for too long . . . We want him to think with us instead of for us.'
Source: Quoted by Paula Giddings in *When and Where I Enter, 1984.*

Even during the Second World War, when the need for military aircraft was at its height, the President of North American Aviation could still say:

'While we are in complete sympathy with the Negro, it is against company policy to employ them as aircraft workers or mechanics . . . regardless of their training . . . There will be some jobs as janitors (caretakers).'
Source: from Philip S. Foner, *Women and the American Labour Movement*, 1980.

Mary McLeod Bethune talking to Mrs Eleanor Roosevelt, wife of the President of the United States in 1937. The two women worked together to try and improve conditions for blacks in America. Mrs Bethune was particularly concerned to improve opportunities for young people.

with great passion and sensitivity what it was like to be black in America. This literature contributed to the growing sense of black pride which was encouraged by some of the more militant black groups. One of the most successful black businesswomen, Madame Walker, made her fortune by selling beauty products specially designed to suit black hair. By 1910 she employed 5,000 black women to sell her cosmetics around the world. Other black businessmen and women proved that they could manage a company as profitably as anyone else, even if few white people ventured into their shops or offices.

Many black people sought comfort in religion, especially in the rural south. Black-run churches were in the forefront of welfare and educational schemes for black

people. There were also campaigning organizations, many of them run by forceful and capable black women, which fought against the unequal treatment of blacks. Rosa Parks had been secretary to the president of her local branch of one of these campaigning groups, the National Association for the Advancement of Colored People, for several years before her arrest. Individual black politicians also made their mark. In the 1930s, President F. D. Roosevelt invited one of the most influential black women campaigners, Mary McLeod Bethune, to join his 'new deal' government team to rebuild the nation after the economic crisis of the 1920s. Mrs Bethune wanted black people to play an active role in national politics. But she was not prepared to force the pace of change. Slowly and carefully was her motto.

Slow progress

It was a Friday evening in December, 1956. Rosa Parks had spent a busy week. She worked hard at her job, but her weekly wages were only $23. That was not enough to support her and her sickly, out-of-work husband, so she did dressmaking in the evenings and at weekends to help make ends meet. This Friday, Rosa had been shopping. She was no longer young, and her arms felt tired after carrying the heavy bag of groceries to the bus stop. Wearily, she rubbed her aching feet. She hoped the bus would be along soon. At last it arrived. Thankfully, Rosa climbed aboard. She paid her fare to the driver, climbed down the steps again and walked around to the door at the back of the bus which black people had to use. Only white people were allowed to board the bus by its front door.

The bus was crowded but Rosa managed to find a seat in the section set aside for blacks. A few stops later, some white people got on to the bus. All the 'whites only' seats were full, and one white man was left standing. 'Get up!' yelled the bus driver to the black passengers. He tried to force Rosa and three other black people to give up their seats and stand for the rest of the journey. Reluctantly, Rosa's fellow passengers got up, but Rosa stayed firm. Why should she stand? After all, she had paid her fare like everyone else. The bus driver was furious. 'Nigger, move back!' he ordered. Again, Rosa refused to give up her seat. What followed next happened very quickly. The police came and Rosa was bundled off to gaol. In the months and years that followed, black people throughout the United States joined in her fight for equal rights. Rosa's quiet defiance started a mass movement.

Rosa Parks was typical of the many 'ordinary' people, both blacks and white, who took part in the mass campaigns for civil rights in the USA during the 1950s and 1960s.

A warning to black people not to vote, for fear of the consequence:
'Staying away from the polls will be the best way to prevent unhealthy and unhappy results . . .'
Source: Southern newspaper, the *Jackson Daily News* (Mississippi) during the 1950s.

From a southern politician during the 1950s:
The Negro has much the same disposition to live without working that his ancestors had in the jungle over 10,000 years ago . . .'
Source: Manning Marable in *Race, Reform and Rebellion,* 1984.

Rosa Parks had seen many changes in the position of black people during her lifetime. In many ways, their situation in the years that followed the Second World War looked promising. The threat of a mass march on Washington in 1941 had forced the government to outlaw any kind of discrimination in the weapons and aircraft industries. Black and white trade unions began to work together. Black women, especially, found a wider range of skilled or professional jobs opening to them. These new black wage-earners formed an important market for manufacturing industries, which turned to producing consumer goods (cars, washing machines etc) once the war was over. Even if half the black population were still living in poverty, this increased black buying power meant that black people were taken more seriously by politicians. As one Southern writer put it: 'We have managed to reduce lynchings not because we're more law-abiding

Above, 21 December, 1956. For the first time, black and white passengers board a bus together. Inside, the seats are no longer segregated; black and white people can sit side by side.

Right, the black singer Marian Anderson was barred for a long time from operas and concert halls. She won great respect throughout the world for her singing during the 1940s and 1950s.

or respectable but because lynchings are such bad advertising. The South is going after big industry at the moment, and a lawless, lynch-mob isn't going to attract very much outside capital.'

Prosperous professional blacks began to be treated as social equals by white people doing similar jobs. In the 1940s, the first black senator and the first black judge were elected. People in high places began to fight discrimination. Even the President's wife resigned from the exclusive white women's society, The Daughters of the American Revolution, because it had refused to allow the black singer Marian Anderson, to sing in its concert halls. But despite these advantages, the position of many black people were still not equal to that of the majority of whites. In 1949, the average income for black families was only 51% of the average for whites. At work, 90% of higher-paid jobs were taken by whites. About 15% of black housing was run down, compared with about 3% of white property, and 40% of black houses lacked an indoor water supply. Rosa Parks' own experience convinced her that there was a long way still to go towards equality.

In the public eye

In the years that followed Rosa Parks' protest, America was engulfed in a series of civil rights campaigns and violent, racist reactions to them. Why was this? Firstly, Rosa's protest came at a time when her local black civil rights organization was geared up for action. The Montgomery branch of the Women's Political Council, a black campaigning group, had been planning to fight another case of racial discrimination on the local buses only a few weeks before Rosa's protest. They had not gone ahead with the case, but they had made many preparations and had gathered numerous supporters to their cause.

Secondly, the Montgomery black leaders' decision to call for a boycott of the buses after Rosa Parks was taken to gaol received wide local support. Blacks refused to travel on the buses for over a year. Usually, the buses carried thousands of black passengers to work every day. Black students organized a system of

car-sharing to get people to work. Their solidarity encouraged the leaders of the boycott to continue campaigning.

Thirdly, the protesters were backed by the local black church leaders, including the man who later became the figurehead of the whole civil rights movement, the Rev Dr Martin Luther King. His vision of a future society with equal rights for all inspired people far beyond the Montgomery city boundaries. His preaching persuaded many white people as well as blacks that the civil rights cause was a just one. Martin Luther King's views were based on the religious belief that all people were created equal. Other black-led movements also provided inspiration for the civil rights campaigners. In Africa, many black states were winning freedom from their former colonial masters. In the USA, more extreme black movements, like the Muslims led by Malcolm X, strengthened black people's pride in their own worth and in their ability to win the struggle for equality.

Rosa Parks having her fingerprints taken by a sheriff in 1956.

BIOGRAPHY

1914 Born into an ordinary black family in the Southern states of the USA.
1920s-1930s Receives a good education.
1940s Joins civil rights organizations in Montgomery; becomes secretary of local National Association for the Advancement of Colored People.
1950s Works in a tailor's shop and as a dressmaker in the evenings to supplement her low wages, in addition to her political campaigning. She also has to care for her semi-invalid husband.
1955 Refuses to give up her seat on a bus to a white man. She had previously been turned off a bus for defying the driver. Is imprisoned, and put on trial.
1956 Arrested again as one of the leaders of the black campaign to boycott segregated buses in Montgomery.
1960s Continues to work for civil rights movement.

Fourthly, Rosa's example of non-violent direct action was soon followed by students, who organized a series of sit-ins at whites-only cafes, cinemas, shops and bars. By April 1960, less than four years after Rosa's protest, over 50,000 students, both black and white, were involved in peaceful demonstrations. CORE and the students also ran campaigns to encourage black people to register their vote. (Unless they did this, they lost their right to vote, but blacks were frequently threatened with violence if they tried to register.) Even though all these activities were non-violent, the campaigners were frequently brutally attacked by whites. Many demonstrators were injured, but this did not stop the campaign. The vast number of people involved in the civil rights campaign and the violence of the white attacks, especially in Birmingham, Alabama in 1963, finally forced the government to take action, and the Civil Rights Act was passed in 1964. It outlawed segregation, once and for all, but it could do little to change white people's attitudes, or to improve the economic position of many blacks.

In this way, all these later stages in the civil rights movement grew out of the bus boycott which followed Rosa Parks' brave act of defiance, rather like ripples spreading across the surface of a pond after a stone is thrown into the water. Rosa's action was important in other ways, too. She was poor, black and female. She worked to support her family. She was typical of the ordinary men and women who took part in the civil rights movement, and stood up to an unjust system in order to fight for equality.

▰▰▰ACTION

1) Contrast the views of women from the Witness box on page 24 with this opinion of black people written by a white man: Blacks were, he thought, *'cut off from the spirit of White society' . . . (they) had . . . 'regressed to a primitive and thus criminal state.'* Paula Giddings, quoting from T.N. Pages' *The Plantation Negro as a Freeman,* 1899.

2) What does the quotation on page 27 tell you about the obstacles facing black people in their fight for equality after the Second World War?

Right, a civil rights march in 1966 being broken up by armed highway patrolmen. The clouds are teargas. The mass civil disobedience campaign was seen as a threat to law and order by the police, even though its aims were peaceful.

❝❝ WITNESS

Here is how E. D. Nixon, one of the leaders of the Montgomery bus boycott, described Rosa Parks: *'She was morally clean, and she had a fairly good academic training . . . she wasn't afraid and she didn't get excited about anything . . .'* **Source:** Paula Giddings in *When and Where I Enter,* 1984.

Martin Luther King writing from jail on 16 April 1963 said that: *'the purpose of non-violent action was not to evade or defy the law.'* "One who breaks an unjust law must do it openly, lovingly", 'King insisted'. "I submit then an individual who breaks a law that conscience tells him is unjust, and willingly accepts the penalty by staying in jail to arouse the conscience of the community over its injustice, is in reality expressing the very highest respect for law." **Source:** Quoted by Manning Marable in Race, *Reform and Rebellion,* 1984.

❞❞

In March 1965, 15,000 people assembled outside the White House in Washington DC. They were protesting against illegal racial discrimination in the south.

31

ANTI-APARTHEID

A divided land

It was after midnight on 16 May 1977. All night, Winnie Mandela had heard strange noises outside the house, but thought nothing of it. She was too busy working on her sociology project. The police were always patrolling the streets of Soweto, the black township outside Johannesburg where she and her daughter lived. All of a sudden, there was a tremendous noise outside, as if a hail of stones or bullets had landed on the roof. Then fists hammered on all the doors, walls and windows, and dogs bayed at the door. Outside, the yard was full of armed men.

'Come out!' they ordered. 'You're under arrest!'

Why did the South African authorities arrest Winnie Mandela? In order to answer this question, we need to look back into the history of southern Africa. The original inhabitants of the southernmost part of Africa were the Khoikhoi people. Over a thousand years ago, other black peoples, including the Zulus and the Xhosas, also moved into the region from the north. The lands were fertile and their crops and livestock prospered. The peoples who lived near the coast traded with Portuguese merchants who sailed to the Cape. News of this 'fine and generous' land soon

spread to Europe, and in 1652 a group of Dutch farmers arrived, determined to settle. They soon drove the Khoikhoi people from their lands, and turned some of them into slaves. Gradually, the Dutch settlers, or 'Boers' as they called themselves, took over more and more land. And as they moved northward, they clashed with the Zulu and Xhosa peoples. The Boers believed that they had a God-given right to live in Africa, and to use the black Africans as their slaves. Not surprisingly, the black Africans fought back. The British also tried to seize a share of the land, partly to settle there but also because they wanted to mine for gold and diamonds. In the 19th century, Africa became a battlefield as the

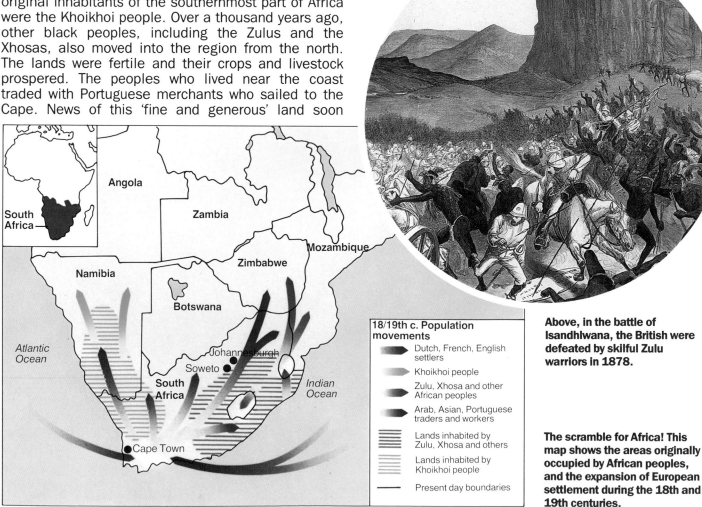

Above, in the battle of Isandhlwana, the British were defeated by skilful Zulu warriors in 1878.

The scramble for Africa! This map shows the areas originally occupied by African peoples, and the expansion of European settlement during the 18th and 19th centuries.

18/19th c. Population movements

- Dutch, French, English settlers
- Khoikhoi people
- Zulu, Xhosa and other African peoples
- Arab, Asian, Portuguese traders and workers
- Lands inhabited by Zulu, Xhosa and others
- Lands inhabited by Khoikhoi people
- Present day boundaries

Angola

Zambia

Mozambique

Zimbabwe

Namibia

Botswana

Atlantic Ocean

Johannesburg
Soweto

South Africa

Indian Ocean

Cape Town

In 1977, Winnie Mandela was exiled to the small white town of Brandfort. The South African government hoped that this would make it difficult for her to continue her campaign against apartheid.

different groups fought for control of the land. In 1910, under British guidance, the former Dutch colonies were granted independence, and became the Dominion of South Africa. The effect of this was disastrous for everyone except the Boers and the British settlers.

In 1913 an act was passed which granted 88% of the land to the Boers and the British. The rest of the land was poor and would not support the black African people, and so they were forced to work for the white settlers. Wages were low and living conditions were often appalling. Except for the inhabitants of Cape Province, black people could not vote, and had no say in the country's affairs.

In the years that followed, conditions for the black Africans became even worse, as the political system known as apartheid (apart-ness) was developed. Winnie Mandela, her husband Nelson, and many other black people joined the African National Congress and fought against apartheid. They wanted equal rights for all people in South Africa. To the government, this was like fighting against the country itself. That is why they arrested Winnie Mandela and thousands like her.

"WITNESS

Nelson Mandela recalls what the elders of his people told him about life in Africa before the coming of the white settlers:

'Then our people lived peacefully, under the democratic rule of their kings . . . Then the country was ours . . . the country belonged to the whole tribe. There were no classes, no rich or poor and no exploitation of man by man. All men were free and equal and this was the foundation of government. The council was so completely democratic that all members of the tribe could participate in its deliberations. Chief and subject, warrior and medicine man, all took part and attempted to influence its decisions.

There was much in such a society that was primitive and insecure, and certainly could not measure up to the demands of the present epoch. But in such a society are contained the seeds of revolutionary democracy, in which none will be held in slavery or servitude, and in which poverty, want and insecurity shall be no more. This is the inspiration which, even today, inspires me and my comrades in our political struggle.'
Source: Statement by Nelson Mandela during his trial in 1962.

The apartheid system

'Apartheid' means 'apart-ness'. According to the South African government, its policies towards the different groups of people living in South Africa are designed to cater for each group's separate needs. But many people believe that this is not the case. They argue that those policies are really designed to benefit white people only. In their view, 'separate' development has not meant equal development: they claim that all 'non-white' — black, coloured and Asian people living in South Africa have suffered under the apartheid system.

On page 32, we saw how most of the land had been given to white people after the state of South Africa was set up in 1910. This deprived most black people of their traditional way of earning a living: farming. Instead, if they wanted to earn money to feed themselves and their families, they had to work for white people. Often, they were given hard, dirty and poorly-paid work to do. In the years that followed, laws were passed which worsened the conditions of black people still further.

Under these laws, everybody who lived in South Africa was 'labelled' by the government, according to race. There were four groups: Blacks, Asians, Coloureds (an offensive term for people of mixed race) and Whites. These racial 'labels' affected almost all aspects of peoples' lives. Marriage with someone from another racial group was not allowed by law. Separate areas were marked out by the government for black, white, coloured or Asian housing. You could be arrested if the police found you in one of the 'wrong' areas without permission. Many shops, restaurants, parks, swimming pools and even public libraries were reserved for white people only.

Education and medical care for whites were far better than for other races. Even ambulances were segregated (divided) into those for whites and those for blacks! Trained black people, for example doctors or nurses, received lower pay than white people doing the same jobs. Often, it was hard for black young people to get any training for a job at all. A few of these unfair rules have been relaxed in recent years, but there is still a long way to go before blacks are treated equally with whites.

The South African government also tried to remove all 'non-white' people from areas that were officially white. To do this, they set up 'homelands' or 'Bantustans'.

Some white South Africans have also campaigned to end apartheid. Here, two of the leading anti-apartheid campaigners, Antony Heard, left, editor of the Cape Times newspaper, and Helen Suzman, an opposition MP, are shown talking to Dr Nhato Motlana, of Soweto black township.

Left, a hostel for black miners, 1986. These men come from the black homelands, and from neighbouring countries, to seek work. They have to leave their wives and families at home and live in these cramped surroundings for 49 weeks each year.

Below, many black women work as nannies or as domestic servants for white families. Like the mine-workers, they often have to leave their families behind, to be cared for by relatives.

Black and coloured people were forcibly removed from their old homes, and taken to resettlement camps to await transport to their new 'homeland'. These supposed homelands were far away from where most black people used to live and work. The government established them in the most remote and barren parts of the country, where there were no jobs and where the soil was often too poor to grow enough food. In 1970 all black people were made citizens of one of these homelands, and deprived of their South African citizenship. This meant that they no longer had any right to a say in how South Africa was governed. In the 1980s their South African citizenship was restored, but the threat of being sent to the homelands remained.

Gradually, many black people have moved back to white areas to try and find work. This is against the law, and they are often arrested and imprisoned. Because black people are needed to work in the cities, the government allows some of them to live in 'townships', or in special hostels. White employers sometimes provide a room for their servants. But workers are not allowed to bring their families with them from the homelands, and so many children are brought up by relations, and see their parents only once a year.

In the homelands and townships, living conditions are poor. Houses are small and crowded, often without electricity, running water or proper sanitation. There are few public services, such as telephones, and very few doctors, schools or hospitals. Life is even more grim for black people in the illegal squatter camps where many stay while trying to avoid being sent to the homelands. There, houses are often rough shacks, made of scrap metal and wood. In the summer the ground becomes a sea of mud. Disease and death are common, particularly among children.

❝ WITNESS

Ellen Kuzwayo, a black writer, describes life in the black township of Soweto:

'. . . the majority of parents leave every morning, some of them as early as four o'clock, and come back home late in the evening. . . . Most parents leave their children sleeping . . . The average monthly wage for men is between 200 and 350 rands a month . . . Within the first week of the month, this meagre wage dwindles fast into rent and electricity accounts which never come to less than R75. The basic monthly food bill comes to at least R95; and this is a true example of living from hand to mouth: the food in such a home is mainly mealie-meal, one vegetable a week, fresh or sour milk every other day, and other basic needs like fuel, water, soap. The cheapest monthly third-class ticket to work is R15. The rest must cover essentials such as medical charges, children's school uniform, school and book fees, as well as shoes and warm clothes in winter for the family. The replacement of other necessities, such as household linen, becomes a luxury. There is never any money left for entertainment, and there may be endless admonishment from the priest for unpaid church dues. . . Poverty on this scale co-exists with a white standard of living that is among the highest in the world.'
Source: Ellen Kuzwayo's autobiography, *Call Me Woman*, 1985.

35

Opposing apartheid

The scene is Soweto black township. A little girl, about 8 years old, raises her hand in a black power salute as a 'Hippo' troop carrier rumbles past. Then: 'The Hippo stopped and opened fire on that child. On the Saturday we went to the mortuary and found the body of the little girl . . . riddled with bullets.' From *The Guardian*, 5 December 1976.

The Soweto children's riots of 1976 are one of the most well-known, and horrifying, episodes in the struggle against apartheid. No-one knows how many children were killed in clashes with the police and army, but some witnesses put the figure at 500 or more, with thousands injured. The children rioted because the government passed a law saying that, in future, all lessons for black children were to be taught in Afrikaans, the hated language of the white Dutch settlers. But the children had another, deeper, reason for protesting. They knew that under the apartheid system they had no chance of receiving as good an education as white children. They rioted because they wanted equality.

The Soweto children were not the first people to fight against apartheid. The South African National Congress (later the African National Congress, or ANC) had been formed in 1912. It campaigned by peaceful means: petitions, deputations to parliament and protest meetings. In 1948, after the Nationalist party came to power and introduced many laws which discriminated against black people, Nelson Mandela and others formed a 'Youth League' of the ANC and organized a campaign of peaceful protest against these new laws. Over 8,500 people were arrested and imprisoned. In 1955 the ANC organized a mass meeting called 'The Congress of the People'. South Africans of all races attended, and proclaimed a 'Freedom Charter'. It began with the words: 'South Africa belongs to all who live in it, black and white.' Other organizations, from the Asian, white and coloured communities, allied with the ANC to fight for equality.

Peaceful demonstrations against the government continued, and were met with violence. In 1960, at Sharpeville, 69 people were killed and 176 were wounded when the police fired into a peaceful crowd of men, women and children. The whole world was shocked; there were demonstrations in many countries, and calls for a boycott of South African goods. The government outlawed the ANC, and arrested thousands of anti-apartheid campaigners, of all races. In 1961 an armed branch of the ANC was formed, called 'Spear of the Nation'. Nelson Mandela went to Europe and to other African states where he met leading politicians and asked for their support in the struggle against apartheid. In 1962 he returned to

Men and women run for their lives as the police fire at them in Sharpeville, 1960.

South Africa, and was arrested. In 1964, as a result of a campaign of sabotage (destruction), organized by 'Spear of the Nation', Nelson Mandela and six others were sentenced to life imprisonment. Winnie felt, she said, as if 'part of my soul went with him.'

Other protesters, black and white, continued the struggle. Students at South African universities staged marches and sit-ins; there were strikes and protests in the townships. In the 1970s, Steve Biko organized the Black Consciousness movement to fight for better lives for black people. He was brutally murdered in prison in 1977. There have been more riots. White writers, journalists and researchers have also campaigned against apartheid. One of the most famous, Ruth First, was killed by a letter bomb in 1982. The government's reply to all these protests was to declare a state of emergency in 1985. Now it is illegal even to report the protests. In South Africa you might be arrested for reading this book!

Above, Nelson Mandela trained as a lawyer, and, before his trial, worked to help black people in need of legal advice. This picture shows him in the office he shared with Oliver Tambo, now leader of the ANC.

Right, a protest by black supporters of Nelson Mandela and the other ANC leaders during their trial. The posters made the protesters' message very clear.

WINNIE MANDELA

The early years

Winnie Mandela remembers her childhood:
'I remember her (my mother) asking God every day for a son. This also developed in me the feeling, I will prove to her that a girl is as much of value to a parent as a son.' from *Part of My Soul,* 1985.

Winnie Mandela was born in Pondoland, in the Transkei. She was one of nine children. Her mother died when she was young, and she often had to take time off school to help look after her baby brother and to work in the fields. Her family was poor, and life was hard. Winnie did well at school, and went on to study at a social work college in Johannesburg. She became the first black woman to qualify as a medical social worker. In Johannesburg, Winnie met many others who were campaigning for a better life for black people. Some were members of the ANC, others had joined the Trade Union movement. After her marriage to Nelson Mandela, she began to share in his political activities.

In Winnie Mandela's own words, 'We became such total comrades in the struggle.' She joined the ANC Women's League and then, when the ANC was banned, the Federation of South African Women. In 1958, she took part in a women's demonstration against apartheid, even though she knew that she would be dismissed from her job if she were arrested. She did lose her job. Since then, she has often found it very difficult to get work. She claims the security police visit

A rather formal portrait of Winnie Mandela, probably taken for publicity purposes. Winnie Mandela has had to become used to living in the public eye as a result of her campaigning activities.

❝ WITNESS

Winnie Mandela has been gaoled and tortured many times. Here she describes life in prison:

'The first few days are the worst in anyone's life — that uncertainty, that insecurity; there is such a sense of hopelessness . . . the whole thing is calculated to destroy you, not only morally but also physically. You know the enemy could keep you there for five years, you are not in touch with anybody. And in those days all I had in the cell was a

sanitary bucket, a plastic bottle which could contain only about three glasses of water, and a mug . . .
The days and nights became so long I found I was talking to myself. It is deathly quiet — that alone is a torture. You don't know what to do with yourself . . . the cell is so small you can't even run right round. . . You find yourself looking for anything in the cells. For instance, I remember how happy I was when I found two ants, how I spent the whole day with those ants, playing with

them on my finger and how sad I was when the warder switched off the light . . .'

Winnie Mandela's daughter, Zinzi, describes her:

'She's a very sweet person, but when she gets into those fights with the police, it's bad, you know; she's got a hell of a temper.'
Source: Winnie Mandela, *Part of My Soul,* 1985.

Women carrying buckets of water and heavy bundles of firewood in one of the black homelands set up by the South African government. Many men from the homelands have to leave their wives and families in order to look for work.

her employers and threaten them. Winnie has praised the numerous friends and colleagues who have helped to support her while Nelson has been in prison, often at great risk to themselves.

Before he was taken away to prison, Nelson warned his wife that the years to come would be hard for her. Like all non-white South Africans, Winnie Mandela has had to struggle against apartheid, which denies equal jobs, housing, schooling and welfare to black South Africans. Like many wives of migrant workers, or children of black servants, she has had to cope with the pain and loneliness of a lifetime's separation from the husband and family she loves. As a black woman, who was brought up with the traditions of her people, she has had to learn how to become a public figure, with political views of her own, even though she knows that many black men still hold the traditional view that a woman's place is in the home. The government have banned her, imprisoned her, tortured her and slandered her. Her family and friends have been harassed. Even the family dog was poisoned. Her children were refused schooling. Eventually, with the help of foreign diplomats, Winnie was able to send them to a boarding school in the neighbouring country of Swaziland. Her hopes of a career and of a normal family life have been completely destroyed.

Winnie Mandela and her children. Winnie has had to take responsibility for providing for her family, while her husband is in prison.

Few other people could stand up to such pressures, but somehow, Winnie Mandela managed to continue to fight for her ideals. Nelson Mandela has spoken admiringly of her 'iron will'. Winnie herself claims she has been helped and inspired by the example of other anti-apartheid fighters, and strengthened by her visits to Nelson in prison, and by the letters that he is allowed to send her twice a year. Above all, she says, 'I look forward to some day — even if it will mean just a day — enjoying some kind of married life with him.' Her belief that Nelson Mandela will one day be free is the greatest inspiration of all. Even so, 'Nelson's release on its own is not the issue,' she says, 'we are struggling for the freedom of our people.'

WINNIE MANDELA

In the public eye

Winnie Mandela has come to stand for the struggle for black equality in South Africa. Numerous friends and colleagues have described her courage, her willingness to listen or help, and her strength in enduring the long separation from her imprisoned husband. Like Nelson Mandela, she has chosen to live a difficult life rather than betray her ideals. She is clearly a remarkable woman. But, from the point of view of the government of South Africa, she is also a criminal. She has been tried and found guilty on many occasions of breaking the laws of the land by refusing to follow the rules of behaviour for black people laid down by the apartheid system. To many people, inside and outside South Africa, those rules seem cruel and unjust, but they are still the law. Defiance of the law raises an important question: can it ever be right to disobey laws, even if those laws are bad laws?

Throughout history, people have been prepared to stand up for what they believe to be right, and to campaign for change. Winnie Mandela is one of those people. How can we say whether we think her defiance of authority is right or wrong? One way is to look at the ideas that she and the other members of the African National Congress (ANC) believe in, and think about whether we believe in them too. Another way is to look at the apartheid system, and see whether we think it is a good, just or fair system of government.

Winnie Mandela's campaign for equality with other races raises another important question. Even if we decide we agree with the aims of Winnie Mandela's campaign (and most people today think that apartheid is unjust), then do we agree with how she fights to achieve her aims? In 1964, Nelson Mandela and his colleagues were imprisoned because they decided that the time had come for the black people to use violence as part of their struggle for equality. *The Times* newspaper called them 'men goaded beyond endurance': that is to say, they had been driven to violence because the South African government refused to listen to their peaceful demands for equality.

More recently, Winnie Mandela has made a rousing speech in which she said that Africans would be driven to use violence to get rid of their enemies. Later on however, she claimed that she had said this to show the strength of her feelings and not to encourage people to commit murder. Winnie Mandela's courage has inspired many people. But her stand against apartheid also raises many issues for us to discuss.

Winnie Mandela and mourners giving the black power salute at a funeral in Soweto. Many blacks, adults and children, have died in clashes with the army and police in Soweto since 1976. Winnie has been criticized for not condemning violent demonstrations against apartheid. What do you think? Can violence ever be justified?

❝ WITNESS

From Sally Motlana, imprisoned with Winnie Mandela in Johannesburg:

'Despite the hardships in her life . . . she was forever ready to listen, to smile, to comfort. To me, a leader of that nature is a great leader.'

From Bishop Manas Buthulezi:

'. . . "the Mother of the Black People". I am not saying this simply because she happens to be the wife of her husband, who is one of the imprisoned leaders of black people, but also *because of what she has become in her own right.'*
Source: Winnie Mandela, *Part of My Soul*, Penguin, 1985.

From the South African government's Minister for Justice:

'I . . . am satisfied that you engage in activities which endanger or which are calculated to endanger the maintenance of public order . . .'
Source: Winnie Mandela's banning order. 23 December 1976.

A rare photograph of Winnie and Nelson Mandela together, taken before Nelson's life imprisonment in 1964. They have spent most of their married life apart. Before his arrest in 1962, Nelson was so busy with campaigning that Winnie said 'a life with him was always a life without him.'

///ACTION

Winnie Mandela's courage has inspired many people. Her stand against apartheid also raises many issues for us to discuss.

Imagine that you are a member of the non-violent branch of the African National Congress. You meet friends who tell you that they have joined Nelson Mandela's branch of the Party, called 'Spear of the Nation'.

Your friends say that they are prepared to use violence to fight apartheid if necessary. You do not agree. In fact, you are shocked and horrified.

Ask your friends to tell you why they have decided to use violence. Make them give you their reasons. Then put forward your own arguments against violence in reply.

BIOGRAPHY

1934 Born in a small village in Pondoland, Transkei. Winifred, a German name, was added by her father, who admired the German people for their strength and capacity for hard work. Her father came from a line of local chiefs, but chose to work as a teacher. Later, Winnie Mandela said that he had introduced her to the ideas behind the struggle for black liberation:
'When my father taught me history, I began to understand.'

1952 Moved to Johannesburg to train as a medical social worker. Became first black woman to qualify.
1958 Married Nelson Mandela, a respected lawyer and a leading figure in the fight for black equality.
1958 Imprisoned (while expecting her first child) for taking part in a black women's demonstration against pass laws.
1962 Nelson Mandela arrested and, in 1964, sentenced to life

imprisonment for taking part in a sabotage campaign.
1962 Winnie 'banned' to a restricted area.
1962–1977 Frequently arrested and imprisoned, sometimes in solitary confinement. Continued to campaign and to work for black welfare.
1977 Banished from her home in Soweto (a black township) to Brandfort, a town in the white Afrikaner 'heartland'. She refused to be intimidated and continued to defy the authorities.

1977–1979 Her house at Brandfort frequently raided by police (sometimes twice a day) and Winnie often arrested.
1979–1985 Continued to campaign; frequent clashes with the government.
1985 Her house petrol-bombed. In defiance of the police, she moved back to Soweto. Was forcibly moved out by the police.
1986 Continued to try and live in Soweto, and to take part in black campaigns for equality.

Conclusion

All three of the women whose lives have been discussed in this book have fought for equality. They have chosen different targets to attack, and different ways of fighting for what they believed in, but they have all been convinced that people — men and women, black and white — have a right to be treated equally before the law.

Millicent Garrett Fawcett campaigned for women to have equal rights with men to vote for members of parliament in Britain, and thus to have a say in how their country was governed. She believed that patient, reasonable argument was the best way of convincing men that women could be 'trusted' with the vote, and refused to take part in any violent or potentially illegal demonstrations. Rosa Parks defied laws that she believed to be unjust, and, at the end of a long campaign of mostly peaceful protest, involving millions of other Americans, she was eventually proved right. Winnie Mandela is still fighting for equality between black and white people against the unjust apartheid system in South Africa. In doing so, she has had to break her country's laws, and be punished for doing so, many times.

These three women have come from different countries, with different beliefs, languages and traditions. They have come from very different social backgrounds, and the experience of their everyday lives has been totally dissimilar. Over a hundred years separates Millicent Garrett Fawcett's first public meeting from Winnie Mandela's latest demonstration. And yet, despite these differences they have a lot in common.

They have all been determined and courageous. They have all worked alongside other people, men as well as women, in organizations which shared their aims. Their home and family lives have sometimes had to take second place to their campaigning work. They have all had to endure organized opposition to their activities, which has sometimes been violent. They have all had to face times when they felt that they might never manage to achieve their aims within their own lifetime, although all of them have had faith that, because their cause was just, it would eventually succeed. They have all shared a vision of a better future for the people around them, and have had to make difficult decisions about the best way of turning that vision into reality. Above all, each of them has had the power to inspire others to join them in working together to achieve equality.

BOOKS TO READ

BRITAIN
Books for adults but recommended reading:
Women's Suffrage in Britain 1867-1929 M. Pugh, Historical Association Pamphlet, London, 1980.
Women of Ideas, Dale Spender, Ark Paperbacks, 1983.
Strong-Minded Women, Janet Horowitz Murray, Penguin, 1982.
Women in Public — the Women's Movement 1850-1900, Patricia Hollis, George Allen and Unwin, 1979.

Millicent Garrett Fawcett wrote several books. Two, written late in life are:
The Women's Victory — and After: Personal Reminiscences, Sidgwick & Jackson, 1920.
What I remember, T. Fisher, Unwin, 1924.

Emmeline Pankhurst also wrote her autobiography:
My Own Story (1914) reprinted: Virago, 1979. A contemporary account of the fight for votes for women is given in: **The Cause** (1928), Ray Strachey, reprinted: Virago, 1978.

SOUTH AFRICA
Winnie Mandela's autobiography is essential reading: **Part of My Soul,** Winnie Mandela, Penguin, 1985.
Call Me Woman, Ellen Kuzwayo, The Women's Press, 1985.
Mother of a Nation, Nancy Harrison, Grafton/Collins, 1986.

An account of the Soweto riots of 1976 is given in:
The Child is Not Dead, British Defence and Aid Fund for South Africa and the Inner London Education Authority, 1986.
Children Under Apartheid, International Defence and Aid Fund for Southern Africa in co-operation with the United Nations Centre Against Apartheid, London, 1980.

USA
Difficult but essential reading:
When and Where I Enter, Paula Giddings, Bantam, 1985. A much simpler book, which looks at the fight for civil rights in America is:
Civil Rights in the USA, People Then and Now, Maureen Montgomery, Macdonald, 1986.

Background information:
Americans, Desmond Wilcox, Delacorte Press, 1978.
United States of America, Macdonald, John Bear, 1974.
A Matter of Colour: Documentary of the Struggle for Racial Equality in the USA, Lorraine Hansbury, Penguin, 1965.

Documentary evidence:
Black Woman in White America — a documentary history, Gerda Lerner (ed.), New York: Pantheon Books, 1972.

Black women writers:
I know why the Caged Bird Sings, Maya Angelou, (and other books), Virago, 1980-1986.
Brown Girl, Brownstones, Paule Marshall, Virago, 1982.
The Color Purple, Alice Walker, The Women's Press, 1983.

1) Look at Winnie Mandela's description of her time in prison on page 38. Make a list of the words that she uses to describe how she felt, and what she thought about the people who had put her there. What does your list tell you about her feelings? Do you think you would feel the same? Give reasons.

What does the story about the ants tell you about the effects of solitary confinement? What does it also tell us about Winnie Mandela's character?

2) The picture below shows a 'suffragette' (a member of The WSPU — Women's Social and Political Union) being arrested for trying to present a petition to the King at the wedding of Prince Arthur in 1913. Look at the crowd surrounding the woman.

From what you have read in this book about Victorian attitudes to women, why do you think that it is composed mainly of men and boys?

Look also at the clothes worn by the woman who is being arrested, and then compare them with the clothes worn by the working women on page 13. (These photographs were taken at about the same date.)

Do you think that the suffragette was a working woman, or that she came from a wealthy family?

Working women were involved in the struggle to win the vote, and also in the Trade Union movement, but many of the suffragette campaigners came from the middle and upper classes. Can you think of at least two reasons for this?

Time chart

1789 France
The French Revolution, with its demands for 'liberty, equality, fraternity' (or solidarity) between all members of society, brings ideas of equality before the public.

1861–1865 USA
American Civil War, between north and south, ended slavery in the south. But, blacks and whites still did not enjoy equal conditions in many southern states, and women throughout America did not have equal civil rights with men.

1850s—1860s England
A few pioneering women succeeded in gaining entry to male professions, for example **Elizabeth Garrett Anderson,** sister of Millicent Fawcett, who became the first woman to qualify as a doctor in England in 1865.

1865–1866 England
A group of women campaigners drafted a petition, to be presented to Parliament, demanding equal rights to vote for women and men.

1884 USA
Ida B Wells, a black teacher and journalist, fought a court case against the railway company after she had been forced to leave a first-class railway coach because of her colour. Although she lost her case, she continued to fight.

1903 England
Emmeline Pankhurst founded the Women's Social and Political Union ('suffragettes') to campaign for equal votes for women. The suffragettes were prepared to take direct, sometimes unlawful, action to further their aims.

1911 South Africa
Olive Schreiner, a white South African feminist and socialist, published a book, 'Women and Labour', in which she claimed that women throughout the world were oppressed, in their work and in their relationships with men.

1936 USA
Mary McLeod Bethune was recruited to the government team led by President T. Roosevelt, along with other influential blacks. They helped to formulate government policy to provide more equal opportunities for black people.

1954 USA
The Supreme Court declared segregated education unlawful. Black female students were among the first to try to gain entry to former segregated schools and colleges, often bravely facing opposition from whites.

1950s—1960s South Africa
Delegates of all races drew up a Freedom Charter (1955). Many women, from the black and white communities, worked together to oppose apartheid. Among them were **Helen Joseph, Lilian Ngoyi** and **Helen Suzman.**

1970s—1980s South Africa
Violent clashes between male and female anti-apartheid protesters and South African security forces. Pro-black leaders assassinated, including Steve Biko (1977) and **Ruth First** (1982).

Glossary

Afrikaans/Afrikaner The language (or the person who speaks it) of the descendants of the Dutch settlers in South Africa. The government's attempts to teach all lessons in Afrikaans (rather than in English, an 'international' language) sparked off the student riots in Soweto in 1976. Many black people in South Africa refuse to speak the language, because it symbolizes the unequal treatment of blacks by whites.

ANC (African National Congress) formed in 1912.

Apartheid Literally, 'apartness'. The system of 'separate (and unequal) development' set up by the National Party in South Africa in a series of laws passed in the 1950s and 1960s.

Banning A system of restrictions on movement, meetings, etc imposed by the South African government on people who, it feels, are a danger to national security.

Boers Another name for the descendants of Dutch settlers in South Africa. (See page 33).

Boycott An organized campaign to ignore an individual, or a country and its products.

Bussing The practice of moving American children (often from black ghettos) to schools in white areas, and vice versa, to make sure that schools were completely integrated. It was often violently opposed by white parents. (See page 23 and front cover.)

Civil Rights A term used, especially in America in the 1960s, to describe equality in all those areas of a person's life covered by national or local government regulations: for example, the right to vote; the right to equal opportunities in education, jobs or housing; the right to equal provision of public services, such as transport, sanitation and welfare. The Civil Rights campaigners demanded all these rights for black men and women, equally.

Discrimination Literally, choosing. Used to describe political systems or peoples' attitudes which make an unfair distinction between people on the grounds of colour, race, or gender.

Disenfranchisement Denying someone the right to vote, or taking the vote away from them.

Equality Being equal. The women described in this book have all campaigned for equality of different kinds, whether between men and women, or between people of different colours.

Ghetto A separate area (usually a clearly-defined district) set aside for a particular group in society, usually a group that is being discriminated against. It was originally used to describe the Jewish quarter of European cities, but is now also used to describe the black districts of many American cities in the northern states.

Homelands Areas set aside by the South African government for black people

to live. They are often barren and very poor, with few jobs and sparse health care or educational facilities. When the apartheid system was being set up, the government forcibly removed many black people from officially 'white' areas, and transported them to the homelands.

Integration Term used to describe a social system whereby black and white people live together on equal terms, with equal opportunities available to all.

Lynching Illegal execution (by hanging) of black people by whites in the southern states of America.

Plantation A large estate, where crops such as cotton or tea were grown, worked by slaves.

Sabotage A campaign of deliberate damage to property.

Segregation Separateness, usually between black and white people. In America before 1954, and in South Africa today, the segregated schools and other facilities provided for black people have usually been inferior to that provided for whites.

Servility Being like a servant; forced to feel and act like an inferior.

Suffragette A follower of the Women's Social and Political Union led by Emmeline Pankhurst, who campaigned by direct action for women to have equal rights with men to the vote.

Suffragist A campaigner for votes for women, usually,

but not necessarily, a supporter of the National Federation of Women's Suffrage Societies, led by Millicent Garrett Fawcett. Suffragists kept their campaigns within the law, however unjust they believed the law to be.

Townships Black settlements on the outskirts of major South African towns and cities, where black workers live. Some townships are legal, others have grown illegally as blacks have moved there from the homelands in search of work. Conditions in the townships are very poor when compared with the high standard of living enjoyed by many white South Africans.

Index

PLACES TO VISIT

The following organizations may be able to help with additional information. Write to them to ask what services they can offer, and whether it is possible to make an appointment to visit them:

ENGLAND
The Fawcett Library, City of London Polytechnic, Old Castle Street, London E1 7NT.
Commission for Racial Equality, Elliot House, 10–12 Allington Street, London SW1E 5EH.
Afro-Caribbean Education Resource Centre, Wyvil School, Wyvil Road, London SW28 2TJ.
Afro-Caribbean Library Association, Hornsey Library, Haringey Park, London N8 7JA.

USA
There is a library run by the United States Information Service at the American Embassy, 24 Grosvenor Square, London W1.
NAACP (The National Association for the Advancement of Colored People, 186 Remsen Street, Brooklyn, New York NY 11201.
National Urban League, 500 East 62nd Street, New York NY 10021.

SOUTH AFRICA
British Defence and Aid Fund for Southern Africa, Canon Collins House, 2nd Floor, 64 Essex Road, London N1 8LR.
Anti-Apartheid Movement 13 Mandela Street, London NW1 0LW.